victoria

PERSIMMONY

by
Stephen Cosgrove
illustrated by
Wendy Edelson

MULTNOMAH

Other books in this series
Fiddler
Shadow Chaser
Gossamer
Derby Downs
T.J.Flopp
Ira Wordworthy
Hannah and Hickory

PERSIMMONY
© 1990 by Stephen Cosgrove
Published by Multnomah
Portland, Oregon 97266

Printed in the United States

Library of Congress Cataloging-in-Publication-Data

Cosgrove, Stephen.
     Persimmony / by Stephen Cosgrove ; illustrated by Wendy Edelson.
          p.   cm.
          Summary: The riddle frequently muttered by an odd and reclusive otter is finally deciphered by the townspeople, who are then able to offer her the friendship she needs.
          ISBN 0-88070-285-0
          [1. Animals—Fiction. 2. Friendship—Fiction.]   I. Edelson, Wendy, ill.   II. Title.
PZ7.C8187Pc   1990
[E]—dc20   90-6694
                                                                       CIP
                                                                       AC
          91 92 93 94 95 96 97 98 - 10 9 8 7 6 5 4 3 2

Dedicated to Wendy Edelson.
Through her gift others
are able to see the pictures I write.

Stephen

Farther than far and to the very edge of the horizon was a path bordered in lacy fern. If you followed that path in the early spring rains and hopped from puddle to puddle, you would find the Land of Barely There.

Barely There, where in early spring the flowering trees hold their buds so tight, afraid are they to release so much beauty in one tiny place. Barely There, where the last bird of winter and the first bird of spring loudly try to sing the rain away.

    If you followed that path as it wandered through the dripping forest, you would see it change from path to rutted road without pause or reflection. That road wound through Barely There and eventually stopped in the square of a quaint little village.

    The village sprawled upon the

countryside like a lazy man on a couch. Here, a variety of folk whiled their lives away: Ira Wordworthy, the owner of the Mercantile; Beaulah and Beauford, the woodcarvers; and old Fiddler bear, a musician of great reputation.

They all lived here, you know, the rich and the not-so-rich, in odd little cabins and cottages. The rich lived in town, and the poor lived in Humble Hollow at the edge of bare-boned Beggary Creek with its trickling bony fingers of water.

Of all the houses that were built in Barely There, there was none more odd than old Parsimony Mansion. Years before, the halls had rung with music, laughter, and the rhythmic scuffing of dancing feet.

But Parsimony Mansion had fallen on hard times; the windows were now shuttered and the grounds were in disrepair. It had been bought some years ago by a miserly otter called Persimmony Parsnip. She was a very odd otter, for she wore gowns sewn of old printed flour sacks and cornstalk binding.

An odd place, old Parsimony Mansion, lived in by an odd Persimmony Parsnip, whose life was a mystery . . . a riddle.

If Parsimony Mansion was odd on the outside, what lay stored inside was odder still. For Persimmony Parsnip was a saver, a finder of all things discarded or sold beneath value. There were old rough-woven blankets, patched and scratchy, stacked high. There were cans of this and cans of that, labels faded and dusty.

Her crinkling skirts rustled down dusty halls, as with lantern held high she would take inventory of her possessions, searching for something misplaced. As her worn slippers shuffled, she often muttered these words, *"I close my eyes and look around. I look and look but it can't be found."*

Newspapers, cardboard, balls of string . . . all were counted and cared for in this odd mansion by this odd otter. She added to her treasures daily, for she was always on the move, searching, searching. And the riddle was that she didn't know for what she searched.

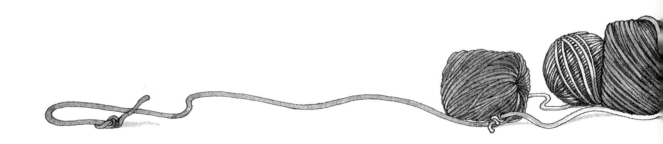

On any given day, Persimmony could be found looking and looking for that which she could never find. The kindly villagers tried to help her in her search, but when they asked what she was looking for she always answered the same: *"I close my eyes and look around. I look and look but it can't be found. Do you know what I am looking for?"* Then, with a shake of her head, off she would wander looking here and there.

What could she be looking for? No one knew and everyone asked.

"Tsk, tsk," they would say as she shuffled by. "Poor, old Miss Parsnip!"

If the truth be known, she was anything but poor. In fact, it could be said that she was the richest of the rich. Persimmony chose to clutch her wealth in worn, little hands, and she had made her richness her poverty.

So life went on in Barely There—
summer and fall. In the springtime, the rains
fell and moistened the land, long parched by
cold winter winds. Barren, dried clods of poor
earth became rich when touched by this
wealth of rain. This year was wealthier than
most as the rain tried to drown the sorrow of
winter past.

As lightning flashed and thunder
cracked, the folk of Barely There rushed
quickly from overhang to porch. Even

Persimmony moved more quickly, as she held
an old newspaper above her head to shed the
downpour.

Like all things, a little can become a lot.
Creeks became streams became rivers
became raging torrents, and just like that the
land was flooded. Oh, and it was frightful!
The river oozed at first like molasses over
griddle cakes, and then it flowed faster still as
all the land became flooded.

The river filled with uprooted trees and displaced folk who sadly sat on twisted tree limbs like floating spectators at some festive event. This was not, however, a festive event. This was a frightening flood of monstrous proportions.

As the waters receded, all went back to a sense of normal as neighbor helped neighbor clean up the mess. Some were not so fortunate as others. Down in old Humble Hollow, Beggary Creek had flooded its banks in a way no one could have expected.

Not one, not two, not even a few of the
rickcty homes survived the raging waters.
Every humble home had been washed away.
Even the Heart family, who had built their
shack upon a great stump, were wiped out . . .
devastated. No clothes, no food, no shelter.
Everything was gone.

The townsfolk took them in, one and all, and no one was abandoned. But there were so many families and so few empty places where they could stay. Even the porch of the Mercantile was used, and makeshift beds were strewn about like firewood on a hearth.

But it was not enough as more and more were rescued. Finally, everyone gathered on the Mercantile steps to discuss their plight.

"We need food and blankets. We need shelter. Oh, what are we to do?"

It was then that Fiddler, a wandering musician of some repute in the Land of Barely There, remembered Persimmony Parsnip and the things she had collected and stored. Without further ado, he sloshed through the mud to old Parsimony Mansion.

With muddy prints left on bleached silvered steps, Fiddler rapped on the door. After a time there came the clanking of bolt and lock being opened.

Persimmony looked out suspiciously through the door, for few had come to call before. "What do you want?" she croaked, as she clutched her tattered shawl.

"Miss Parsnip," he said, hat in hand, "we need your help. There was a terrible flood and folks have no home, nor blankets to keep them warm. Won't you open Parsimony Mansion and take some of these folks in?"

Her eyes rolled as she muttered those familiar words, *"I close my eyes and look around. I look and look but it can't be found.* Do the homeless have what I have been searching for?" she asked with knitted brow. "If they do, they can come. If they don't, they all can stay away." With that, she rudely slammed the door.

Fiddler rushed back to the store, and with everyone gathered about he told them what the old otter had said.

"What does this riddle mean?" asked Father Heart. *"I close my eyes and look around. I look and look but it can't be found."*

Everyone thought and thought the whole night through, thinking of anything and everything that might be the answer to this riddle. They thought it might be an old brooch. They thought it might be a lost

pocket watch. All were eliminated as Fiddler
rushed to ask Miss Parsnip if this or that was
what she was looking for.

All was to no avail, for Persimmony
answered each question with the self-same
riddle.

It was late in the night, so late in fact that it was nearly morning, when from the back of the store stepped Fiddler. "I know the answer. I know what she needs and what she has been searching for. It is so simple that even she has disguised her need in the searching."

With all the villagers and the folk from Humble Hollow gathered around, Fiddler told them the answer to Parsnip's riddle.

Dawn's purpled light bathed the village in an eerie glow as everyone marched down the street to Parsimony Mansion. Once there, Fiddler rapped loudly on the door once again. The group hushed. All could easily hear the shuffling of slippered feet and the crackling rustle of Persimmony's printed dress. Locked bolts were slammed back and the door squeaked open.

"Miss Parsnip," Fiddler asked once again, "folks have a need for a roof over their heads and blankets to keep them warm. Won't you take them in?"

The odd otter looked over the crowd and grumbled, *"I close my eyes and look around. I look and look but it can't be found.* Do you know what I am looking for? If you do, you can come in. If you don't, you all can stay away."

Then to her surprise, one at a time, they came forward and whispered in her ear and gave her a quaint little hug. Without hesitation and with a gentle smile upon her face, Persimmony Parsnip let them in.

That day they changed the name of Parsimony Mansion to Charity Hall, for it was soon filled with grace and the laughter of all who lived inside. What was the secret to Persimmony's riddle? What had old Miss Parsnip searched for all her life that was whispered to warm her heart?

They gave no gift nor money to lend. They simply said, "We'll be your friend."

And that is what we all endlessly search for . . .

in the Land of Barely There.